MW01517774

# Zen *Shredding*

# Zen

•

# *Shredding*

[Insights, Questions and Confessions of a Meditator and Novice Snowboarder on the pursuit of dreams, inspiration, passion and change.]

*m* sean symonds

Edited by Monika S. Ullmann

Order this book online at www.trafford.com/07-2662 or email orders@trafford.com
Most Trafford titles are also available at major online book retailers.


Note for Librarians: A cataloguing record for this book is available from Library and Archives Canada at www.collectionscanada.ca/amicus/index-e.html

Printed in Victoria, BC, Canada.

ISBN: 978-1-4251-5887-3

*We at Trafford believe that it is the responsibility of us all, as both individuals and corporations, to make choices that are environmentally and socially sound. You, in turn, are supporting this responsible conduct each time you purchase a Trafford book, or make use of our publishing services. To find out how you are helping, please visit www.trafford.com/responsiblepublishing.html*

*Our mission is to efficiently provide the world's finest, most comprehensive book publishing service, enabling every author to experience success. To find out how to publish your book, your way, and have it available worldwide, visit us online at www.trafford.com/10510*

**www.trafford.com**

**North America & international**
toll-free: 1 888 232 4444 (USA & Canada)
phone: 250 383 6864 • fax: 250 383 6804
email: info@trafford.com

**The United Kingdom & Europe**
phone: +44 (0)1865 722 113 • local rate: 0845 230 9601
facsimile: +44 (0)1865 722 868 • email: info.uk@trafford.com

10 9 8 7 6 5

In the gift of your Soul ~ Magic.

In the expression of your desire ~ Song.

In the solitude of your heart ~ Freedom.

In the body ~ God.

*Dedicated to those who pursue the wisdom of their Soul*

# C o n t e n t s

# Acknowledgments

*To* my teacher Deepak Chopra, I cannot express in words the gratitude and honor it is to share in the gift of your wisdom and knowledge. Your voice and heart has woven the thread of its influence and freedom easily within the pages of this book and my life. Thank you for following the path of your own unique journey while sharing it so generously with others.

To my editor Monika S. Ullmann, your contribution has been a brilliant addition to the vision and expression of this work. Thank you for tending this “garden”, with so much clarity, candor and compassion!

To Louise Thompson and Ora Ray, thank you for your continued friendship over these many years. The courage and conviction you have so easily expressed in your life has influenced and inspired me deeply in unforeseen ways.

And to Glenn Iles, Kelly Oswald, Nicole Walleen, Mom and Dad and the folks at Trafford publishing for your contribution to this project ~ supporting me in the creative expression of my life.

*And* to the many unspoken hero’s and heroines in life; our teachers, mentors and snowboard coaches who continue to restore the memory of knowledge, wisdom and playfulness in us all.

# *Zen:*

The practice of seeing deeply into the nature of things through direct experience and awareness.

# *Shredding:*

A slang snowboarding term describing the art of "tearing" up a snow surface with skill, tact, timing and coordination...

# *Sutra:*

Sanskrit term meaning "thread". A sutra is a short pithy statement that can generally not be understood without some sort of commentary or direct experience. The goal of any Sutra practice is to unravel or penetrate the meaning of a Sutra through contemplation and the direct experience of meditation.

# Introduction

*Sometimes* we just need to show up. When we spontaneously show up we often have an opportunity to take the time to experience our lives in new and exciting ways, perhaps for the very first time. When we show up, we create the opportunity to learn more about the gifts, talents, dreams and passions we have. We allow the Spirit in our life to move through us in ecstatic ways. When we have an opportunity to share our gifts, talents, dreams and passions we also have the ability to engage change creatively while discovering more about the mystery of who we really are and who we can become.

*I believe* human beings crave inspiration, and the intent of this work is to inspire you to cultivate inspiration and change in your life. It is my hope that these words and insights will ignite your own passions and support you in cultivating the pursuit of your own dreams. I believe many of us have lost touch with the value and meaning of inspiration and the effect it can have on our life. The word inspiration comes from the Latin word Spirare, meaning Spirit; to infuse with an encouraging or exalting influence; to animate or give life; the stimulation by divinity and genius. We ignite the fire of inspiration within us by getting in touch with who we are while also cultivating and pursuing the dreams we were born with. As we discover who we are and get in touch with those dreams I believe almost anything is possible. When we are inspired change occurs at a very organic level and we approach and experience life from a place where Nature nurtures us.

*Most of us* have been conditioned to live life in very conventional ways of being many of which are based on struggle. I believe that our world would be a completely different place if it was filled with human beings who lived their lives more actively in the pursuit and cultivation of inspiration, while also discovering who they are. When we surround ourselves with people who inspire us, mentors that lead us, teachers that support us and experiences that nurture our Soul at a very deepest level, effortless change becomes the natural way of living and Being in life.

*When you witness* the experience and story of someone who genuinely enjoys life, you will often find that they have taken time to uncover, refine and express an inner inspiration that ripples as passion into all their relationships. There is no more important task for us than to pursue and experience deeper levels of inspiration in our life, to look directly into the mystery of our being and embrace it wholeheartedly. This has been an underlying theme and hunger in my own life and the lives of a few inspiring people that I have had the honor of meeting and befriending. This is not a book in any conventional sense of the word. In January of 2005 another birthday rolled around for me and I decided that it would be an auspicious time to learn how to snowboard. For someone living in Whistler, B.C., one of the worlds foremost winter playgrounds, this would seem like an obvious choice. I'd simply reached a point in my life where I was tired of standing on the sidelines; I didn't want to watch others playing any more, it was time for me to play. The intention behind the choice was simple: I wanted to bring more inspiration into my life, to push some personal boundaries, to get back into my body, to enjoy the freedom and bliss of being in the body, on the mountains, while playing in the snow.

*I have pursued many passions* in my life, the most important being my Spiritual Journey. During the last twenty years or so, I have been blessed with experiences that have dramatically changed the way I see and experience my life. Sometimes simple choices have a way of weaving new experiences and possibilities into our lives. My immersion into my snowboarding adventure is in its third season as I type these words in the fall of 2007. On the surface Zen Shredding is a fusion of different experiences and different worlds. Zen Shredding is a culmination and synthesis of my ongoing Spiritual Journey, expressed as insights, filtered through the experience of snowboarding. I hope it truly inspires you to push your own boundaries, to take risks in the journey and to discover who you are.

*Since this is not a conventional book,* let me make a few suggestions that could enhance your experience and understanding of this work. While you could choose to read this as a book from cover to cover, my suggestion is that you don't! Perhaps after reading the introduction you might progressively make your way through each insight, one at a time. As an approach you might simply read the insight and stay with it for a day and note what it brings up for you. Perhaps the next day you would read the explanation and commentary I have written and again, see where it takes you. Finally, you might ask yourself the question to anchor it into the everyday reality of your life. Whether you choose to stay with the experience of one insight a day or week, feel comfortable with your own rhythm, get to know your own rhythm. Using this somewhat unconventional approach, I think you will find a deeper appreciation for the value and impact the insights and book can have on your life by intentionally making it a process rather than a read. Journaling all of these steps will also deepen and enliven your experience. I continue to work with most of these insights as they have served me well in my life. I trust that some may serve or even inspire you in your own journey of transformation and change while on the path of discovery to the one divinity and humanity that lies within us all.

*On a final note I need to confess* that I have taken artistic liberty in borrowing the term Zen for the title of this book. I am not a practicing Buddhist nor am I a Zen meditator. I have been meditating daily since the fall of 1989 and over those years have been exposed to knowledge and experience that has lead me to the belief that all meditative practices when successful have the potential to lead us to the same "destination". My affinity with the title, its basic definition and the archetypal representation of the Buddha, encapsulates for me a fleeting state I have touched; it speaks directly to a way of being I seek to cultivate.

*Thanks for showing up.*

Michael Sean Symonds

October 12th 2007

*This is a book about life questions and answers...*

*In the course of your life you will ask yourself many questions. To know where you are heading you just need to listen to the questions you are asking yourself in every moment.*

*Sometimes when you ask questions you will receive a response to every situation as it occurs and other times you might need to sit with those questions, to accept the unresolved questions of your life unconditionally as part of the mystery of your life experience. Most of us spend our lives looking for answers and happiness outside ourselves and are never really satisfied. Many of us also ask questions that dwell only on the practical necessities of life and as a result live lives of mediocrity. As you practice asking questions you will learn to navigate not only the mystery of your Soul but also the journey of your life. Knowing which questions to ask is part of the mystery and creative challenge of being. Some of the most important questions you can ask are:*

*Who am I?*

*What do I want?*

*Why am I here?*

*These three questions will eventually merge to*

*become one;*

*What am I doing for others and how can I contribute more to the planet I live on?*

INSPIRATION

DREAMS

OPPORTUNITIES

*Harnessing your dreams to your life is a life-long process*

For many years, *I could only come up with the reasons that prevented me from taking my first steps in learning how to snowboard. In my heart I could imagine what it would be like to experience the joy and freedom of sliding down the mountains, I just could never "find" the motivation or time to actually take the step. Prior to learning, I used to walk to the base of the mountain and watch the snowboarders as they shredded their way to the bottom. I've also been to San Diego and one of my favorite pastimes there is to go out to the end of a pier and watch the surfers as they wait patiently for the swell of a perfect wave.*

*There's something mystical and meditative about the whole process of simply being with elements of nature. There is serenity in the focused way each surfer reads the potential and possibility within the seed of an oncoming wave. We don't have an ocean in Whistler, but we do have over 33 feet of snow a year. When you blend the backdrop of jaw dropping scenery, fresh snow and bluebird skies together a canvas of white trails provides adventure and quietude that can elevate your Soul. Watching those surfers and snow boarders made me long to be part of it. I've always intuitively felt that envy was a positive emotion, a signpost that I had stumbled on a truth that desired expression within the story of my own life experience. Eventually, this feeling became strong enough to motivate me from being an observer to becoming an active participant.*

You are never too old or too young to pursue a dream.

A fulfilled life is the continued realization of dreams and the pursuit of passions. Your intentions and desires, however wild and exotic, are there to inspire you. They are the keys to personal and global transformation.

*What do you dream of being, doing or having, what aspirations do you have for your life?*

Great dreams have
an incubation period.

Sometimes your most important dreams and desires will take time to manifest. To let those dreams and desires unfold naturally and spontaneously, you need to be completely detached from the who, what, where, when, how and why of life.

*Are you willing to let go of the who, what, where, when, how and why of your life?*

Take action on your dreams.

There is no magic genie to fulfill every wish, want, need or desire you have. By taking small, simple steps towards your future in the present you engage the creative process at its deepest level. As you take action by stepping into the unknown, you engage the flow of potential in your life and in this flow lie all possibilities.

*What small action step do you need to take towards the realization of your fondest dreams?*

It doesn't really matter what you believe.

While circumstance, situation, skill and talent can shape the perception of your process and outcome, there can be no causal connection between your practice, belief and outcome. It is only the perceived obstacles of your life that are deeply affected by your practice and belief.

*What perceived obstacles do you have in your life that prevent you from experiencing a deeper level of success or the pursuit of your dreams?*

Your dreams are the way.

It's so easy to defer to external sources for solutions to quell the hunger and passion that screams inside. While prophets, sages and seers may provide needed or necessary information, pursuing a dream ~ any dream, is the first step in orchestrating a life of deeper fulfillment and meaning.

*Do you trust the still, small voice within you?*

Pursuing dreams is
not just about
achieving something.

It's also about "letting go". Pursuing a dream often generates change and transformation that nudges your life in quantum leaps.  Stepping into the unknown is less threatening when you detach from expectations and old ways of being that no longer serve you.

*What behaviors or beliefs do you need to let go to pursue your dreams?*

Life is truly what you make it.

Whether you're four, twenty-four or sixty-four, you will always have the ability to learn something new. Creating an experience that provides growth, transformation and pure joy isn't age dependent.

*What will you create today?*

Live the dream.

You will always be able to come up with reasons to kill your dream, to become a victim of your own reasoning. You were born to live the dream; you were born to be the dream.  When you hold back on the dream, you resist the creative expression of the entire Universe.

*How do you victimize yourself and your dreams with excuses?*

Why not.

If you're the kind of person who has struggled with decision-making, it might be time to practice the 'why not' principle. This principle means you don't have to have a reason for doing something. To have a reason is to justify. You don't have to have a reason to be, do or have something. Sometimes you simply know without knowing why.

*What meaningful choices do you ignore in your life?*

Inspiration is the essence of fulfillment.

Whatever you do, lead with inspiration. When you are inspired, you will have the strength and fortitude to pursue your life even during the most challenging moments. Surround yourself with people who inspire you, live in places that nurture you. Take a moment each day to notice the perfection and inspiration that is present all around you. Immerse yourself in the inspiration that lives inside you.

*What can you do to stimulate your inspiration?*

Seize opportunities.

But what opportunities? Find the opportunities that hide in the people, places and experiences that occur daily in your life. The opportunities that lie dormant in the conversations, chance meetings, and relationships. The most important thing is to pay attention to the story of your life, listening and looking for relevant themes and continuity. Every moment is potentially an extraordinary moment.

*What opportunities in your life need to be pursued?*

# LESSONS FROM THE BUNNY HILL OF LIFE

*It's about falling down,getting up, learning*

*It's six am. I'm getting up early not only to meditate but also for some serious snowboard lessons on a Whistler/Blackcomb bunny hill. A couple of years ago I had a false start to my snowboarding adventure. One lesson combined with all too icy surfaces quenched my thirst to be short listed as the next Olympic hopeful. This time around it feels different; my adventure unfolds magically providing me with not only the basic skills needed for a potential lifetime of successful riding, but also a boot camp opportunity to return to many insights that have shaped the journey of my own life.*

*Conventional reality suggests we live life in linear ways. We go to school, learn specific subjects, graduate, go to college and university and then we start "to live our perfect career and life". But is this really true?*

*It's an affront to me that so many people are taught to muffle, ignore and deny the whispers of their own inner voice. It's sad that many people spend large portions of their life and income denying their inner wisdom that could lead them into a lifetime of meaningful experiences filled with passion and purpose. While it took a couple of years for me to move past the initial judgments and fear I had around my first experience of snowboarding, the voice of desire could not be ignored. The commitment to take more lessons helped buffer the doubts and fears that had kept me paralyzed. It was an important reminder to pay attention to what called me and to nourish and cultivate the seeds of my dreams.*

*As my learning journey continues in my snowboarding adventure, I often see many novice snowboarders foregoing formal lessons. If they only knew that a few simple insights, suggestions and skills could greatly influence their degree of pain or success. Practice and technique provide the skills necessary to express the unbounded creative potential we were born with. By choosing to take lessons based on progression, I was able to navigate my momentary experience in little chunks of challenge that had options within opportunity and clearly defined beginnings, middles and endings. While there were moments where I felt overwhelmed, the support of an instructor and the familiarity of the bunny hill allowed me to learn and play at the same time.*

Start life on the bunny hill.

Our greatest teachers are often the most successful learners. Children learn as they play. If your learning does not seem playful something might need to shift in your life.

*What needs to shift in your life?*

Take some lessons.

We are all intentionally hard wired for Nirvana; a lesson or two with a good teacher will gently support you in the direction of your most treasured dreams.

*What do you want to learn?*

Take some lessons from life.

Our greatest evolutionary path is occuring in the present moment. What needs to be taken care of in your life is reflected directly by what is going on or not going on in your life.

*Are you succeeding in fulfilling your life?*

Life is your teacher.

If you believe you are here to learn lessons, life itself can provide you with more than enough to contemplate. Paying attention to your own experience can elevate your process, as does the realization that observing others in their own process is much less painful than recreating the same lessons over and over again, personally.

*Does your current reality inform you or determine you?*

It’s OK to fall.

Pursuing happiness often leads into circumstances and situations that make you feel derailed. Sometimes you just need to stop, take a breath and recapture your focus ~ in most cases the pain is only temporary.

*If success were guaranteed for your most important dream, what would you do?*

Recognize struggle in your life.

Most of us have been conditioned to believe that we must struggle, strive and work hard in order to achieve or be successful. When you recognize struggle you can choose to momentarily pause and pull back your attention from that struggle.  This creates space and within the space you will find the freedom to choose a different way of Being.

*What areas of your life feel like they are a struggle?*

If it feels like push, it's probably time to play.

When your favorite ways of being no longer generate joy, consider that you may be hitting an unrealistic barrier of compulsive expectation. While discipline sometimes enhances the success of your commitments, it's often in the moment of play that you will find your greatest insights, breakthroughs and inspiration.

*Do you force yourself to 'do' life?*

Be gentle, be effortless, and be easy.

Find the rhythm of your own life. When you live according to your own rhythm you'll also have connected to the greater universal rhythm. Then your life will flow with effortless ease. Be gentle in your mind, be effortless in your body, and be easy in your Spirit.

*How can you be gentler, easier and more effortless in your life?*

It's fine to feel like you're not good enough.

New circumstances can often place you in situations were you feel inadequate and inferior. While these inner programs and conversations often repeat themselves over and over again in your life, it's valuable to recognize their insignificance to who you truly are. Reminding yourself that you are not your emotions, thoughts, feelings and beliefs is a way to navigate the more challenging inner terrain of the mind that may often hamper or debilitate the pursuit of your dreams.

*Is it time for you to change the inner conversation you're listening to?*

Find your “hot spots”.

It's amazing how easy it is for us to forget what is important and meaningful. When you look at your life do you think about how unhappy and unfulfilled you are? When you take the time to remember which activities, choices or experiences bring you the most fulfillment and then cultivate more of the same, you'll often find yourself being re-inspired by your own life and decisions.

*Where are your 'hot spots' and which ones are missing? What activities, choices or experiences could bring more fulfillment and inspiration into your life?*

To be or not to be.

Most of us spend our lives seeking happiness but never really find it. We create elaborate plans with lofty goals that may or may not serve us. It's good to plan and it's good to have goals, but true freedom and joy can be ours if we learn to simply observe the moment as it unfolds.

*How would you live your life if you knew the who, the what, the where, the why and the how were already taken care of?*

Show up.

So many journeys and dreams are cut short before they even begin. As your mind slices and dices your experience, you can lose yourself in the confusion. Learn to mute dissection, analysis and judgment of your life experience and simply show up. Having done that, you can step aside and allow the moment to unfold.

*When was the last time you remember just showing up for life and how did it feel?*

Do more of what you value.

Life does not have to be a complicated affair. While there are so many different trails you could take sometimes spending more time on the ones you already enjoy is the best route.

*What do you value most?*

Life is a web of relationships.

When you spend time in Nature, it's easy to recognize the interdependence of all things. You can see that the trees filter air, which turns into moisture, which nourishes the earth, that cultivates the seed, which once again becomes a tree, a simple example of the infinite number of possibilities woven into the tapestry of our life. Every experience is intricately connected with a thousand invisible threads that bind and tie, link and nurture us. Doting on details is redundant, recognizing the relationship is paramount.

*Does the story of your life define and perpetuate your independence or reveal and inform you of your interdependence?*

Make promises to yourself.

Most of us are very good at making commitments to work, to life, and yes, to the relationships we value the most, but how often do you make promises to yourself? How often do you take the time to examine with clarity what you need to live life with more passion, joy and fulfillment?

*What promises do you need to make to your Self to live life with more passion, joy and fulfillment? What do you value most?*

For “it” to happen you need to step aside.

You are not the doer: you are an instrument, a vehicle, and a vessel. The more you show up and step aside in the moment, the more you will experience the exhilaration, the passion, the inspiration and joy of simply being.

*What would your life look life if you knew that success had nothing to do with planning or rehearsing of the moment?*

Slowliness is holiness!

In your fifteen minute sound bite of stardom, finishing first, fastest, smartest, most skilled or best in the class will only last as long as it takes for the Universe to catch on that it's time your ego got refreshed with a face shot of purifying, fluffy snow!  Take your time in life; the how, what, where, when, why and who unfolds naturally as you remain attentive to the moment.

*How can you make your life less busy?*

# LISTENING LEARNING PLAYING

*It's about seeking and finding our purpose, our people and our pleasure*

*I could never have imagined or dreamed that learning to snowboard would have such a profound impact on my life. While it may have initially provided an alternative outlet to experience more pleasure and play in my life, it has unexpectedly filtered directly into many other threads of my life experience and creative process.*

*Being in Nature you will find places that excite and inspire you, that speak deeply to your being.*

*When I first experienced Seventh Heaven on Blackcomb Mountain, it felt like I had stumbled across the perfect place for me to simply* be. *I look for those 'aha' moments, the environment, the people, places and experiences that seem to fit perfectly, like hand to glove. In those moments it does not seem like they are just experiences that have happened outside of me, but instead, expressions and extensions of something very familiar and very deep within me.*

*I'm now at a place in my life where I realize I don't have to wait for those aha moments to happen, that I can cultivate them gently with quiet attention and detachment. While the mind wants to judge every experience we have as good and bad, the creative process of life accepts all experiences unconditionally. The information and energy of those experiences will eventually be digested, metabolized and transformed into something new and valuable, serving us in completely unpredictable ways.*

Quest out of bounds.

While it certainly can feel safer to stay within the confines of a routine that is predetermined and planned, a mundane, repetitious life can stifle your Soul. Sometimes you need to take responsible risks, to dive into and meet the unknown head on. Sometimes you need to shake up your routine by adding new ingredients to spice it up. When you dive into the uncertainty of these moments the magic and mystery of life will often roll in ecstasy at your feet.

*Are you stifling yourself and your Soul with too much routine and repetition?*

Play is an all too often neglected discipline in life.

While the ski hill trail signage of blue and black may lead to a great adrenaline rush, a return to the ease of a green run will remind you just how far you have come.

*How can you play more often in your life?*

There is only one purpose ~ the continued expansion of happiness.

According to preference or skill, green, blue and black are flavours to be enjoyed and indulged at will.

*Do you surround yourself with people and experiences that nurture happiness?*

Ask for what you need.

Too often we expect that life will automatically provide what we need to be happy and fulfilled. Most people cannot read your mind, so learn to be comfortable asking for what you want.

*What do you need most, right now?*

There are no mistakes.

While it is tempting to evaluate our lives from someone else's view of how it 'should' be, freedom lies in the realization that all your experiences can eventually inform and contribute to your current perspective on reality. Reality prevails prior to all assessments, judgments and perceptions that you or others may have about life. With acceptance there is no need to forgive. While your experience may be filled with many little deaths, all roads lead to the unified whole.

*What mistakes do you assume you have made?*

Look out for death cookies.

It's unreasonable to think that bad things don't happen to good people. Life will constantly throw curve balls that sometimes bring you to a dead stop. You can never be prepared for these moments, but you can alleviate them with practiced recovery and self care, recalibrating yourself to an appropriate level of balance.

*Do you have a reliable support system of people and practices that nurture you to the depths of your Soul?*

Seek inner affirmation of your Being.

Most of us have been conditioned to seek external approval. True freedom lies in your ability to acknowledge and realize who you are being over what you are doing. When you are able to recognize the only affirmation you need is the sanction of your own inner being and existence, you'll be free to unleash your creative capacities in any direction you choose.

*Whose approval do you seek and why?*

Give yourself permission.

You cannot progress if you constantly hold back. While feedback, guidance and inner reflection are some ways to experience more clarity, sometimes you just need to give yourself permission to do life, to show up and see what unfolds as a result of choices you're making.

*Do you rely on the opinion of others to govern your own life?*

Find your ‘posse’.

Finding and building relationships with a core group of individuals who are big enough to support you with the dreams and desires you have for your life will elevate and accelerate your life experience to new levels of intimacy, freedom, joy and success.

*Do you surround yourself with people who nurture and support you in reaching your highest potential?*

Don’t be dependent on your ‘posse’.

If we put people on pedestals and then expect them to live up to our standards, this often turns into a dose of disappointment. To have friends that value and honor you is a good thing. To imagine that you can rely on someone in all situations and circumstances, indefinitely, is an unrealistic expectation. It's OK to immerse yourself, but detrimental to enmesh yourself in relationships.

*What dependency or attachment do you place on the relationships you value the most?*

# DISCOVERING YOUR SELF: YOU ARE MORE THAN YOU KNOW

*Life is a process of change, discovery, risk and flow*

*One belief I consistently bump up against is the notion that to experience change, transformation or success, there has to be struggle and effort. Throughout my life journey and my experience of snowboarding I was challenged to examine some of my deepest held beliefs in who I thought I was. Who I am is much more than my thoughts, feelings, emotions, memories and perceptions, who I am is more than the body/mind I have identified and become all too familiar with.*

*In hindsight it is easy to recognize that the majority of the barriers I experience are presented by my mind alone and that one key to navigating the terrain of change and transformation is to simply get out of the way and allow it to happen. With practice and some kicking and screaming, I realize the process of discovering who I am is about letting go of my imagined 'me'. When I do that, it creates enough space for something new and incredible to surface, the experience psychologists call 'flow'. At the end of a good day on the slopes I can only have two perceptions of reality: I can imagine that it is some sort of me that determines how successful I may or may not be in getting to the bottom of the hill, or I can do my best at getting out of the way of that imagined me and allow the mystery and magic of my existence to express itself uniquely, naturally and spontaneously.*

Find out who you are.

Finding out who you are is not a shift in perception, belief or lifestyle. While these states can be part of your story, finding out who you are is a revelation, a realization of what you aren't. Every time you identify your Self you limit your Self. Any idea you have about your Self is not your Self. You are not a concept.

*Who are you?*

You are much more than you could ever imagine.

No one shortchanges us as much as we shortchange ourselves. Whether it's environment or conditioning, as long as you continue to see your life from the level of the mind you will experience limitation. Wisdom tradition suggests that as you move beyond the mind by identifying with your true nature, you step into a playground of eternity.

*In what ways do you shortchange yourself?*

There are many levels to your existence.

Most human beings imagine they are just their bodies, their past, their successes or their failures. Some have become more accustomed to exploring a redefined self based on emotions, beliefs, desires and ideas, the concepts of who they think they are. While these layers are ever more refined, they are still only subtle aspects of self that eventually merges into the One, no self.

*Who is it that desires, who is it that believes, who is it that conceives?*

Explore and navigate the terrain of your life.

The essence of adaptability is your willingness to explore and navigate all layers of your existence. Skill can be enhanced as you expose, learn and practice new methods of navigation. If there were such a thing as success it could be defined as your ability to navigate each moment of your existence without the imposition of a specific perception or viewpoint.

*What can you do to explore all levels of your existence?*

Witness the flow of your life.

The current of your life can change in a moment, an hour or in a day. It's important to recognize that at any moment you might need to slow down, be attentive, speed up or simply stop because that is the call of the moment. While this may or may not coincide with your own plans, learning to surrender to the flow of your life will minimize the degree of struggle you may or may not be having.

*Where is the flow of your life taking you ~ do you need to slow down, be attentive, gear up or stop?*

When you find out
who you are,
everything changes.

It was never about changing the world. Nothing ever needed to be healed, fixed or changed. The Dharma of acceptance is the greatest teacher, a humbling instrument that elevates and ennobles who you are. Your role is to become accustomed to the illusion of an ever-changing world that masks the mystery of your never changing Self.

*Can you accept who you are in each moment without trying to change anything?*

Trust and honor your body ~ love your body.

A biological intelligence exists within your body that is smarter than your cognitive mind. Let your body ride the terrain of life. Look after it and it will look after you. Your individual body is your connection to the larger Universal body. To deny your body is to deny your connection to the world, to deny your connection to the world is to deny your connection to the Universe and its underlying unity.

*How can you honor your body with more reverence?*

You are not your emotions; you are are the one who is having emotions.

Most people have not learned to appreciate the true value of their emotions. To embrace your emotions is to engage your energy ~ keeping it in motion. To deny your e-motions prevents them in leading you to what is important. Denial traps energy from motion. E-motions are not the language of your Soul, they are however one of your most valuable tools to maintaining a healthy connection with your Soul, a stepping stone and guide to clarifying your direction. You are not your emotions you are the one who is having emotions. Learn to love, embrace and understand your emotions.

*What can you learn from your emotions, what feelings do you judge the most?*

You are not your thoughts; you are the one who is having those thoughts.

It is said that we have over fifty thousand thoughts per day, every day. The frightening part of this idea is that ninety percent of the thoughts you have today will be the ones you also have tomorrow. As long as you continue to identify solely with your thoughts they will continue to have power and dominion over you. As you practice identifying with your true nature, your thoughts no longer have the power to disempower you in your life experience.

*What is the most negative thought you have about yourself and how does it influence your life?*

Be present in your body.

The easiest way to get out of your head and into your body is through your senses. Nature's intelligence speaks to you constantly through your senses. The more attention you pay to your senses, the more you nurture your senses. What you touch, taste, smell, see and hear can nurture your senses and allow you to become present to the moment as it is.

*In what ways can you develop awareness around your body and senses?*

Pay attention.

In any given moment your life will be calling you, inviting your attention uniquely. Embrace, discover and celebrate what has captured your attention in the moment, it may provide you with just what you need.

*What calls to you, what speaks most to your heart in this moment?*

Enhance your attention: it's all you've got.

Where your attention goes energy flows. Temporary withdrawal of your attention from activity into silence elevates your attention to greater levels of being. Elevated attention leads to elevated awareness from where you can respond to every situation as it occurs.

*What activities can you withdraw yourself from to enhance your attention?*

Everything you need is within you.

Human beings love to seek outside themselves for adventure, romance, and inspiration. Wisdom tradition suggests that we must first seek inside our Selves for the clues to lasting fullfilment. The way of peace, creativity, understanding, power and love are within. Take the time to look within first, and then let your life unfold.

*What are you seeking?*

Follow the trails of
your own life.

However chaotic, frustrating or perfect your life may have been, the present moment is always the turning point in the direction your life is going. So often we minimize the contribution of past experiences ~ 'good or bad' and the effect or link they may have to the present moment or impending decisions.

*What contribution have the 'good and bad' experiences of your life made to the path of your life?*

Engage your own Spirituality.

All too often many of us adopt external methods of appreciating what we can call the mystery of life. While it is valuable to observe, honor and expose yourself to the process of others who have journeyed or are journeying into the mystery of their own life and Soul, you should not assume that it is the only method or way of being. Realization, peace and purity can be found as easily on the slopes of a mountain, an apartment downtown or a cabin in the woods.

*How can you deepen your journey into the mystery of your life?*

Switch is the only
way to ride in life!

Through conditioning and fear, we imagine that there is only one way to live life, one way to see, one way to be, one way to "do" life. There are no formulas, no plans, and no universal methods that work for everybody, the same way, the same time. Flexibility, versatility and diversity of styles, experience, approaches and ways of being, provide the foundation for a life of simplicity and ease.

*Is there another way of seeing, being or doing your life?*

Embrace your process.

In your search for fresh tracks and greener grass you can get caught up in a pursuit of happiness that disables rather than enables. It is for you alone to decide what works in your life. Coming to terms might include your abstention from the habit of romancing the moment with narratives of saintly virtue and Hollywood melodrama.

*Can you give yourself permission to just be?*

# FINDING AND KEEPING BALANCE, ON THE HILL AND IN LIFE

*Finding balance is all*

*After a few months of snowboarding practice, I began to actively seek opportunities to develop, refine and enhance my skills. My initial fear and anxiety gave way to joy and anticipation. Increased confidence in my own abilities provided greater levels of comfort and ease, so I could simply show up and have fun. The flow of time, experience and knowledge began to serve as a gateway of clarity to the rhythm and flow of my life. I decided to participate in a weeklong 'ride and learn' club. It was an opportunity to meet new people, explore new terrain and improve my skills in the process. There were a couple of Australians in our group who knew how to play hard. One was a surfer who had unfortunately hurt his arm while surfing just prior to coming to Canada. He not only had a big heart but buckets of bravado and stamina. As each day progressed he fell again and again on his injured shoulder. But he showed up every day. He justified his unstoppable attendance by the expense of his trip and the boy inside who did not want to miss out for even one moment.*

*It's good to listen to your body. It provides you with relevant guidance to what may or may not be possible. During the first season I learned quickly, sometimes painfully, to listen to my body. I had a pass that provided me with unlimited trips to the hill. I did not have to show up every day to make sure I got my money's worth; I did not need to spend long days on the hill because I was only in town for a very expensive, week long holiday. It was liberating for me to be able to discover and determine my own rhythm of being on the hill, while also recognizing that this rhythm could be enhanced if I remained flexible as it ebbed and flowed through the days, weeks, months and years.*

Engage the moment as it is.

Conditions can change dramatically in your life. While those conditions may conflict with your predetermined agenda, they are as they are ~ or not. In those moments when your visibility is tempered by distraction, being OK with what is will provide you with a heightened level of presence that enables you to navigate your most challenging extremes.

*Can you be present with your conditions without assessing, evaluating and comparing your life?*

Interrupt
ongoing noise in
your life.

On the slope, you can find perfection in silence. Take a moment to notice and enjoy the serenity, simplicity and silence in things, as they are mirrors of your Being. Notice the pauses and gaps in your life; they are your greatest friends, they are filled with potential and possibility. They are the source of your dreams and the connection to your true Self.

*How can you introduce silence as a practice to your day?*

Do your homework.

Having a Diploma, B.A., Ph.D., or Masters, means nothing if you have not applied your gained knowledge into the practicum of integrated, day-to-day living. All knowledge, talent and learning is useless if it's not applied to the functional world of form.

*How can you apply what you know?*

Find balance.

All areas of your life need a certain amount of attention. Balance allows you to navigate the diversity of life's challenges with greater ease. To find balance you need to define for yourself what balance is and then cultivate its value within your life.

*What can you do to enhance the balance you experience in your life?*

Avoid losing yourself in the noise of your life.

The experience of clarity can be cultivated by the reduction and elimination of drama in your life. Learning to navigate life with effortless ease is a learned skill. When your story becomes overwhelming, when the noise of your life experience overshadows the connection of clarity to your inner wisdom, you can quickly lose yourself in the details and noise of life.

*In what areas of your life is there too much noise?*

Be clear about what
you need.

We have been conditioned to believe in the sanctity of taking care of the needs of others first. Learning to practice Self-care first eliminates becoming ungrounded and scattered. When you can take care of your own needs, you will be ready to take care of the needs of others at a level of unmatched success and mastery.

*How can you take care of yourself in better ways?*

Improve your ride.

While knowledge can often serve as a pillar of strength to specific areas of your life, the regular, consistent experience of inner silence becomes a foundation to nurture all of your life.

*Can you be still and quiet in your mind and body?*

There will always be someone 'better' than you.

If you continue to compare, assess and evaluate yourself according to some external person or ideal, you'll never create the space for your own success to be revealed through the value of Self-expression and Self-appreciation. Your success is based on your ability to express your authentic Self without judgment.

*What benefit do you receive by assessing, evaluating or comparing yourself to others?*

It’s good to have boundaries.

Healthy boundaries support you in the expression of your authenticity. Setting a limit on what you accept or do not accept is simply a way of honoring your preferences for Being in the moment. Learn to play safe by having and supporting your own healthy boundaries.

*What boundaries do you need to honor in your life?*

Enjoy the mystery
of the unknown.

While traveling unfamiliar terrain in life can trigger immense confusion and fear, it often provides the space for new ways of Being to be cultivated and eventually enjoyed.

*When was the last time you tried something new?*

...It's OK to fall ~ again.

Remind yourself that life is the coexistence of opposites “up, down, good, bad, happy and sad”; this elevates your choice to place attention on what is important while withdrawing your attention from what is old and stale.

*What memories from your past are no longer serving you?*

There will be moments when everything comes together.

A time occurs when your dreams, desires and practice will merge providing a sweet, fleeting moment of success ~ you "jib" this moment of success and then you move on...

*Have you ever been happy for no reason at all?*

Acknowledge the significance of your smallest achievements.

They become the stepping stones of your fondest memories and your greatest legacies.

*When you succeed in something do you take the time to acknowledge and celebrate your moment of success?*

Try shredding
new trails in life.

External change is instigated by experiencing internal change. Silence cultivates the space for not only new, inspired ways of thinking and being, but also provides the necessary ingredients to trigger transformation at its most primordial level ~ where all creation arises from and subsides to. Every dream begins with stillness, every desire ~ quietude.

*What choices can you make that will lead to new directions of growth and transformation?*

Live life with intention and purpose.

When you live life with intention and purpose, merging your desires with practiced clarity you may find you can navigate your life experience in more detached ways independent of ever changing external conditions.

*What is the purpose of your life?*
*What intentions do you have for your life?*

# Spend more time in Nature.

There is a rhythm, flow (and chairlift) in Nature that connects us to harmony. Spending time in the rhythm and flow of Nature allows our minds, bodies and Spirit to recalibrate to the very same power that creates a baby and orchestrates a Universe. You can have moments in Nature, when everything dissolves into everything else, where there is no "I", "me", or "mine". Being in nature can often lead to spontaneous meditative states that can fulfill you on the deepest, most natural levels of your being.

*When was the last time you went for a walk in the park or looked for a shooting star in the night sky?*

There is only perfection.

Life will become effortless to the degree you are aware of your own inner perfection. As you learn to cultivate this inner perfection by becoming aware of it, you will open the doorway to see an outer perfection that has always been present.

*Can you find the perfection in your life?*

“Shred” the burden of judgment.

Your life could be seen as the creative process in action. Spontaneity is the essence of the creative process; judgment is what comes after it. When you judge yourself or others you temporarily isolate yourself from the effortless flow of the moment and the energy and information it contains.

*What parts of yourself do you sit in judgment of the most?*

# TRUTH, LIES AND OBSESSIONS

*It's about clarity, courage and letting go*

*For many years I had been developing a negative view towards my body. The combination of moving further away from the biology of my youth, and the cumulative diet of morning muffins with lattes and pasta dinners was having its effect. My first few lessons on the hill were reality checks of just how bad things had become ~ I could barely reach over to strap into my bindings...*

*There is something vulnerable and*

*paradoxical about some learning experiences. You show up to learn something new and all of a sudden, the moment is hijacked by memories of your past failures or fears of future catastrophes. There was a moment during my first lesson where my coach had us practice a side slipping technique, where your board is horizontal to the incline of the mountain with both feet strapped in. The skill was practiced first, facing up the hill and then looking down the hill. In both variations we were to hold the hands of the instructor for stability, without looking at the ground or our feet. This skill practice in particular required complete trust, a letting go and relying on another human being ~ not something I'm so practiced at...*

*I will never forget the intense intimacy and security I felt as I held onto my instructor's hands while gazing directly into his eyes. For a brief moment it felt like there was no past or future, for a moment it felt like I was completely present and completely vulnerable to another human being. In that moment I did not fall, in that moment I bridged the fears of my mind to be present in the possibilities of the moment. My choice to surrender to the moment by relying on someone else's support allowed me to digest the skill at hand and a much deeper learning. It was a reminder of the importance to surround yourself with people who are big enough or skilled enough to support you with the dreams you have for your life.*

Mentors *are essentially people you can trust, people that can provide you with alternative information and new perspectives or skills. Having another point of view helps to prevent you from falling into the traps of self engendered thinking and conditioning, behavior or action.*

Ask questions of your life.

Ask questions of yourself, of others, of what you've been taught, of everything you believe yourself to be. It's important to engage and apply the process of inquiry and investigation into your life, to examine all the beliefs that you have about life. Inquiry and investigation prevent denial and resignation. It is the birth of a new narrative based on the present, not the past or future. Your best questions entice the Universe to respond in a dance of co-creation that transforms your subjective experience.

*What part of your own story do you need to question?*

Suffering will be experienced according to the degree and allegiance you have to your lies.

As you learn to look at, acknowledge and dismantle the lies you've told yourself you'll experience greater levels of subjective freedom.

*In which area of your life do you have the greatest freedom and how do you experience this freedom?*

Less is more, more is less.

Human beings often choose to fill their life with endless activities in order to muffle the experience of feeling their own mental and emotional suffering. The trance of endless having and doing creates distraction while numbing the voice of wisdom within you. Ironically, having less of everything can allow you to engage more: more intimacy, more freedom and more attention to apply to the more important details of your life.

*Do you unconsciously fill your life with activity in order to avoid feeling what needs to be felt?*

Truth can contain the
lie of justification.

When you take the time to examine truth closely, it can reveal negative assumptions, associations and beliefs about how you see your life and the world you live in. When fact and fiction fuse, you limit your subjective experience of freedom.

*What do you assume to be true in your life?*

Every complaint is the source of an unmanifest goal.

Many people think that complaining is just plain negative. What's disempowering is to overlook the fact that each and every complaint is also a potential source of happiness, something that wants to be. Every complaint is a request in disguise, a personal recipe for fast tracking you to greater levels of joy and happiness.

*What are your complaints?*

Find what works in your life.

We often have a tendency to focus on what is not working, which often amplifies and perpetuates it. By taking the time to look at what you enjoy doing or being and where your inspiration comes from, you can refocus your attention to what is meaningful and important.

*What is working in your life?*

Pay attention to the story of your own life.

It's easy to get caught up in the vision and dreams of others, the movers, the shakers, the high rollers, but what about your own visions and dreams? Your future; the intentions and desires, the dreams and visions you have for your life, are a unique mix of the known and the unknown. The known is the story of your life; the unknown is a field of infinite possibilities determined only by the quality and direction of your attention.

*Whose dreams or visions are you following?*

Notice any urgency, obsession or impulse you may have.

When you look closely at your own life you'll notice that much of your behavior is actually driven by unconscious tendencies. Dig a little deeper and those tendencies often reveal hidden fears about who you are or who you might become.

*What areas of your life are dominated by a sense of urgency, obsession or impulse, and what are the underlying fears driving these impulses?*

Embrace the great unlearning.

Most of us spend our lives accumulating knowledge of this and that. Whether it's spiritual knowledge, worldly knowledge or the easiest way to slide down a mogul field, there will be a time when all of it will be surrendered as concept only. The one reality exists beyond the level of the intellect and mind.

*What unnecessary knowledge do you cling to?*

All life is a projection.

Once you understand that you have lived your life according to the veil of concepts, you are free to not only examine the practicality of those concepts but also journey to the place prior to those concepts—and that's where the adventure really begins.

*What would your life look like if you lived without preconceived perceptions?*

Sometimes you need to say No.

Sometimes you need to consciously pass on 'lessons' that generate too much fear and anxiety. By returning to the comfort of the bunny hill you may become aware of something that was missed or needed more practice that eventually becomes a stepping stone of confidence and courage necessary for the next step.

*Is there something you need to say No to in your life?*

Courage is not the absence of fear.

It's the choice to take action in spite of fear. How come the bunny hill seems so small now?

*What is your greatest fear?*

Trust the process of your life.

Most of us have been taught to earn trust. Sometimes you just need to step out and trust a person, place or experience, regardless of what fears you may have. Granting trust to the moment can cause radical transformation if you have relied heavily on your own fears to run your life.

*Who do you trust the most and for what reasons?*

Sometimes you need to say Yes to life.

Life is a paradox; sometimes you need to step outside the comfort of the bunny hill to move forward and evolve.

*Suspending your imagined fears, what steps could you make to change the destiny of your present life?*

You will hunger for clarity.

The hunger for clarity can draw you into activity whether it's fresh new powder, a new relationship or another mountain to climb; this craving for yet another experience and adventure may be temporarily satisfying, but never completely fulfilling. Beneath the surface of the doing, having and creating, resides a deeper yearning of the Soul for the clarity and peace of Being, something that experience can never deliver alone. It is only in the giving up of something that we are free to discover everything.

*Can you be in the world and not of it?*

See things differently.

Flexibility can occur more easily when you adjust your perception to see outside a sandbox you may have already created. Conventional thinking is based on the fusion of ideas, beliefs, notions and concepts that induce premature cognitive commitments on your part. To see differently requires you to temporarily suspend your point of view to create space for new ways of seeing, thinking, doing and Being.

*How might you view your particular circumstances differently?*

The end of suffering is the end of “I”.

If you take a look at your fondest memories, those fleeting moments of happiness, you'll find that for that brief moment in time, the 'you' you imagine yourself to be disappeared, however briefly, and for a fleeting moment the bliss of Being bubbled into your awareness.

*What are you doing or being when you are most happy?*

Finding your true Self
is all about losing
your old self.

A great teacher once said everything you know about yourself, you learned from outside yourself. Personal growth and Spirituality is about discovering who you are by finding out what you're not.

*What stories or lies do you tell yourself about how you live your life; are there areas where you're pretending everything is fine?*

We teach people how to treat us!

We are the source of subjective ecstasy and suffering in life. Sometimes you need to recognize the personal contribution you make to the twists and turns your life may be taking.

*Do you feel comfortable with the way people treat you?*

Abandon who you think you are.

Your greatest barrier to fulfillment is the obstacle of a perceived identity. It's the belief in the existence of a subjective "I" with all its wants, needs and desires, a story with a past, present and future. The path of discovery lies not in gaining, achieving or becoming a self that will have more, do more, and be more. Realization is recognizing that less is more. Realization is an embodiment that happens as 'you' gently deconstruct every concept 'you' ever had, to reveal the 'you' that was always there.

*What thoughts, feelings, emotions, ideas, concepts and labels have you outgrown in your life?*

# PARADISE ON THE BOTTOM OF THE HILL

*Being here now; letting go of judgment; accepting life 'as is'*

*Like most things, you can't change the present conditions on the hill. The moment is an expression of what is happening. One of my greatest challenges continues to be the ever-changing condition of the slopes. While those conditions provide ongoing opportunities for skill development, they also provide the fertile ground for hidden frustrations and blatant struggle to surface. What is happening can't be changed, but how you perceive or react to what is happening can be changed. As a 'mature novice' snowboarder, my biggest disadvantage was packing a lifetime of conditioning, especially during the early months of my learning. I was constantly reminded that in order for me to be really present to the moment, to be able to simply have fun, I needed to be willing to see each moment with fresh new eyes, without labeling, judging, assessing or evaluating the significance or insignificance of what was happening or not happening to me.*

*The inspiration and exhilaration of pursuing new adventures and passions can sometimes hide unrealistic expectations of how the creative process of our journey will unfold. I fell a lot during the first few weeks and months of my adventure, sometimes very painfully. While falls subdued the more pleasurable moments of my experience and temporarily caused me to question my commitment, acceptance and practiced non-judgment provided enough space and courage to keep getting up and continue the adventure.*

*In many new experiences there seem to be moments of creative tension where desire and potential brush up against a lack of experience around new skills or technique. Pursuing the dream, expressing the dream, even understanding the dream often requires a willingness to reflect, learn, and pause, to assess and harness the support of all your resources, conventional or otherwise.*

You had a good run and now you're at the bottom of the hill.

Sometimes living life without expectation can create the needed space for change and transformation to happen naturally. Life expands; life contracts. Great freedom lies in your ability to accept unconditionally the perceived duality at the heart of your life experience. It allows you to be in the world and not of it.

*Can you suspend your agenda of perfectionism?*

Approach life with innocence.

The birth of wisdom occurs when you can see the moment as it is. As you get older there is a tendency to walk into situations with preconceived notions, fears and expectations. When you see the moment as it is there is no movement of mind, no polarity, no filter of concept, good, bad, or otherwise. To see the moment with innocence provides a level of flexibility where necessary information can be accessed to navigate the moment with effortless ease.

*What preconceived ideas do you have about your life and the way you imagine it to be?*

Life is not a trend!

While the latest gear and toys may provide you with temporary comfort and compliance to trend, living life according to your own trends based on your intentions and dreams can provide a more permanent experience of clarity and inner confidence that transcends all external camouflage and distraction.

*What do you need to be true to your Self?*

Do your best.

Most of us have been so conditioned to live our life according to someone else's idea of success that we have forgotten or never bothered to explore what it means to be truly successful according to our own definition and ideal.

*How would YOU define your success?*

There is no distinction; there is no separation.

When you spend enough time in Nature and silence you begin to realize that there is interconnectedness, an interdependence between all animate and inanimate things. There is no subject and there is no object. When you're immersed in Nature and in moments of self-created silence, the barriers of the mind begin to dissolve and you can touch, taste and smell the experience of Unity consciousness.

*Can you recognize that interdependence rather than independence defines your life?*

There is no significance.

Human beings love to place significance on what is thought, felt and done. While significance can be a great tool to honor and direct the focus of your attention, it becomes a trap when you become obsessed with the details and circumstances of your life. While each moment can be honored with reverence, spending your day synthesizing concepts about the whys and wherefores of your life can quickly lead to denial, delusion and self-absorption.

*Do you romanticize your life experience?*

Let the mind do what it needs to do ~ stay out of its way.

One can be afraid and yet still act. One can be confused and yet still decide.

*Where do those thoughts arise from, where do those feelings subside to?*

Move beyond all opposites.

Most of us spend our lives dividing up our life experience; this is not living ~ this is math. Transcendence is the ability to move beyond opposites, to experience diversity as it dissolves into the one substance of reality. Transcendence allows you to begin to identify more and more with eternity rather than the potential distraction of its creative expression.

*What would your life look like if you dropped the language of opposites from your vocabulary: right and wrong, good and bad, happy and sad, virtue and sin?*

Life does not have to be an extreme adventure.

Much suffering comes about as a result of living in the comfort of extreme polarities: rich and poor, suffering and joy, pain and pleasure. The hedonist and ascetic are extreme opposites of the same pole. While some of these moments can be an opportunity for the experience of pleasure, getting stuck in a rut and a way of being can bound the unbounded. If your life feels like an expression of extremes, perhaps it's time to get off the swing?

*Do you 'do' life in extremes?*

Learn to appreciate
the relevance of your
own experience first.

When you can come to a place of acceptance of your own experience regardless of the content, past or present, you experience true freedom and the unbounded possibility within the moment.

*Have you come to terms with your past and present?*

Embrace the lover inside of you.

We all have the capacity to give and receive. For this exchange to occur it is important to cultivate an attitude of Self care, first. For this exchange to be complete, it is important to recognize that both the giver and receiver are one.

*What limiting stories have you told yourself about love?*

Fulfillment of desire
is only one step on
the path.

There is more to life than happiness, creativity, joy or purpose. While elevating the journey of your life these experiences will not, in themselves, provide realization. Realization occurs when you begin to recognize the interconnectedness between all things, when you experience the interdependence of all things where there is no 'inner' and 'outer', where there is no subject/object split.

*What will you do when you are happy, when creativity, joy and purpose are already part of your life experience?*

We're here to give and receive.

Many people who come to Whistler (fill in your own home town) simply take. Within you there is already an abundance of unique gifts and talents.

*What can you do to give back to this planet you call home?*

Your happiness is up to you.

While the romance of story suggests that we find happiness in the “outer”, a quick observation of others provides us with a discriminating understanding that happiness is not an ‘outside job’. Whether there are thirty centimeters of “fresh”, or it’s raining top to bottom, your own level of happiness should not be based on the transient experiences of your life.

*Can you redefine happiness based on an internal ideal?*

Success and failure are completely artificial.

We are conditioned to place a greater significance on the value of success to a point of unrealistic stature. While success should not be judged as bad and failure should not necessarily be encouraged, it can be comforting to know that your true being revels in bliss independent of external circumstance.

*Can your new definition of success also include the experience of failure?*

Express gratitude.

Be grateful for small and big things, including the lift attendant who smiles and welcomes you all day long. Good things can be found in your life. These situations deserve your fullest appreciation and gratitude.

*What do you have to be grateful for?*

Be.

Human beings love to dichotomize life. You think you are smarter than God by placing a label of higher and lower significance on every circumstance, situation, person or thing. Ultimately, it will always be your own projection that limits the ultimate reality of who you are and who you can become. In the stillness of a quiet mind there can be no juxtaposition.

*What happens if everything you do is done without a label of significance?*

You don't have to go to India to get enlightened.

The universe whispers to us constantly through our experience. The greatest lessons can be experienced on a bus, with a friend or in conversation with a ten year old on the beginner's chairlift.

*How often do you listen to and honor the messages in your life?*

You don’t need to figure it out.

Like all methods and ways of Being, the search for knowledge can become a trap. Gathering and gaining knowledge while fulfilling too many, remains a conceptual understanding of experience only. Mere comprehension is just the 'booby prize'. While knowledge is valuable, it is the wisdom of integrated experience that is priceless.

*How would your life change if you gave up the pursuit of understanding?*

Forget everything.

Most of us learn what it takes to get to the bottom of the hill once, and then spend the rest of our lives fixated on using the same method or approach. You don't need to wait until you're on your death bed to realize you reached a plateau some twenty or thirty years before. All paths have their traps. When you step into a moment of uncertainty and change without expectation you can free yourself from the story of your past.

*What would happen if you practiced forgetfulness more often?*

The questions and answers are irrelevant.

While we may have become very sophisticated in asking ourselves some very important questions, they are insignificant unless we discover the one Self who is asking the questions...

*Who is it that asks the question?*

# ON BEING CHANGE.

*Ask your friends* or acquaintances a simple question: how do you feel about change? In most cases it will open the door to conversations and stories that can include adventure and drama, joy and suffering and, depending on the emotional level or closure of the experience, many insights around this loaded word. As a teacher for personal growth, I have actively explored, avoided, pursued, cultivated and witnessed the element of change both in my own life and the lives of others for over two decades. In my own personal journey I continue to dance within the dichotomy of this percieved, love/hate relationship.

*While every moment is fresh*, new and filled with possibility, more often than not the filtering of our past experience prevents us from seeing every moment with innocence and as a result we lose touch with the possibilities that could occur in that moment. The chemistry of change, whether it be by choice or force, is the movement of one moment to the next. For most of us, change remains an unconscious mix of raw emotions, memories of inspiration, and fears of past and future. At the deepest level of this spectrum there are polarities of core belief that prevent us from navigating change with grace and ease.

*Zen Shredding is a narrative* of how a simple choice can open the door to experience, expression and possibility. It's also a documentation of the many stories that result from consciously choosing an experience that forced me to face my thoughts, feelings, perceptions and concepts that consistently arise. As the adventure of this story continues to unfold for me, it also continues to actively engage me in the confrontation of personal agreements I have made to my own story around change, which at times serves to distract, derail and trap me within the experience of my past and the perception I have of my present moment.

*The wisdom traditions of India* have always implied that change is the one constant and illusion that continues to be a source of great suffering for humanity. Tradition suggests that within the midst of the illusion of change there is an unchanging factor ~ you. And while we are constantly tempted to 'manage' the infinite ongoing details of change that exist in our day to day circumstances, most of us blindly ignore the ever present stillness or silence within that can act as a source of strength among the storms of change that pervade our life experience. Within the chaos of change we can find stillness and within the stillness, silence. A silence that is pregnant with possibility, a silence that percolates within itself to become the desire of our tendencies for growth, transformation and expansion. Within the stillness there is a latent potential to transform and elevate our experience of change from a place of conflict, pain and struggle to one of creative ease and effortless response. The mystery of who we are consistently provides us with the stepping stones of clues that manifest as our dreams, desires and passions.

*When we immerse ourselves* in the experience of silence within, we have the ability to cultivate, nurture and elevate the seeds of those passions into an experience of change that occurs more naturally and spontaneously. While the insights, questions and confessions of this work are not enough to change the world directly, I hope they provide the space and preamble for change/transformation to occur at the level of our filters where many of our obstacles reside.

# CULTIVATING EFFORTLESS CHANGE IN YOUR LIFE:

*The following seven themes* were initially inspired by a chapter on change in Deepak Chopra's book *Peace is the Way*. They are also an expression of understanding, knowledge and experience I have received on my spiritual journey and relationship as a certified instructor of meditation with the Chopra Centre for Wellbeing. Cultivating a direct experience of these themes allows you to deconstruct old ways of being, creating the space for the birth of new experiences and possibilities.

## *Find purpose in life:*

Wisdom tradition suggests that we were all born with a purpose, a reason why we are here on Earth. The discovery of this purpose has the power to elevate and ennoble your own life and the world around you. As you pay attention to your essence, you have the ability to calibrate it to its creative expression as it manifests in the world of form. Discovering and cultivating your purpose is a powerful way to navigate your life with greater levels of peace and harmony and protects you from being overwhelmed by the many distractions on the journey of life.

## *Be present, redirect your attention from the past and future into the present:*

It's easy to become distracted by the pain of our past and the potential suffering of our future. Our senses are the easiest way to remain grounded in the present moment. Through touch, taste, smell, seeing and hearing, we have the ability to anchor and connect, digest and metabolize the energy and information ever present within the moment. In all Spiritual traditions there are many thousands of tools that can be used to provide greater levels of accessibility to our Being and its experience and expression through our senses.

## *Cultivate a clear vision or cause:*

We are both the creative expression of the universe and its ever changing potential. Within the complex diversity of humankind there is the one unity of Spirit. When you cultivate your purpose, you will experience heightened degrees of creativity, energy and passion and you'll begin to naturally question what you stand for. Your vision or cause will provide you with the inspiration and clarity of how you will be while you are here and to help manifest your purpose and destiny.

## *Express your excellence:*

You were born with gifts and talents. To express those gifts and talents is to naturally express the excellence of your Soul. Take the time to develop your natural potential. Look for mentors and teachers that give you the opportunity to cultivate, experience and express your natural potential to elevated levels. How you choose to serve with your gifts and talents is your calling. To cultivate your potential as your calling is to align and support you in the successful expression of your cause and purpose. The experiences of your past and the dreams you have for your life can often provide valuable information in clarifying the natural evolution of your purpose, cause and calling.

## *Take action steps towards your new purpose, cause and calling:*

Take the time to discover the continuity leading from your past to the present. Engaging your vision with action steps allows you to create the preamble for change to occur that is in alignment with your heart and the expression of your Soul. If you listen closely to your life experience, you'll naturally be guided towards the steps that can activate and orchestrate the expression of your purpose, cause and calling. In your intentions and desires you'll find the seeds of continuity and potential. Your action steps are ways to practice being what you've always been.

## *Rediscover your innocence:*

A spiritual life is the continued expression and expansion of your own awareness and consciousness. As you move beyond the polarities of good and bad, right and wrong, high and low, you will gradually become more aware of the innocence that lies at the heart of every moment, every dream, every vision and every passion. As you begin to trust the nature of your own Being you will begin to experience the natural expression of its value in your life. Spiritual practice and study can escort and enhance you on this journey; these tools allow you to touch, taste, smell, see and hear the expression of innocence in your life.

## *Become Self Referral:*

Self-referral is the spontaneous choice to abandon your reliance, addiction and need to survive based on external circumstances and situations. It is a state of awareness that naturally develops over time as a result of spiritual study and practice. When you begin to find out who you are, you'll realize the mystery within you is a greater source of power and security than the temporary, ephemeral experiences that make up your day-to-day life. Self-referral provides a degree of detachment that gradually increases to the point where you are completely unconcerned with the story of who, what, where, when, why and how of your life will unfold. It's the embodiment of divine indifference, a natural state of Being.

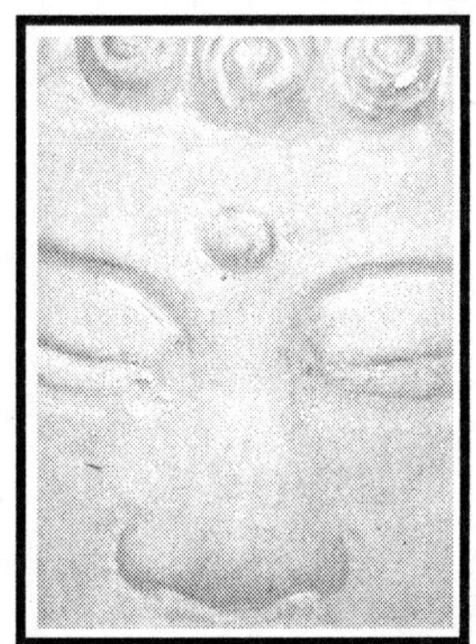

Promises to myself.

*I will practice taking care of my Self first.*

*I will take care not to loose my Self in the noise of my life.*

*I will ask questions only my Soul can answer.*

*I will immerse myself in the mystery of who I am.*

*I will realize the divinity and perfection of the One Spirit that dwells within me.*

*I will listen to my life and my own inner wisdom.*

*I will make choices that honor my Being and realize my dreams.*

*I will validate my Self by who I am being not by what I am doing.*

*I will question all the assumptions I have about myself and the world I live in.*

*I will abandon who I was to become who I am.*

*I will use the gifts I have been given to create the dream I envision.*

*I will work with vision; I will live with passion.*

*I will accept who I am and practice compassion if I 'fail'.*

*I will rediscover my innocence, express my excellence, and serve humanity.*

*I will be the change I want to see in this world.*

*I will meditate at least once a day.*

*I will study the wisdom traditions from all ages.*

*I will remind myself to play, often.*

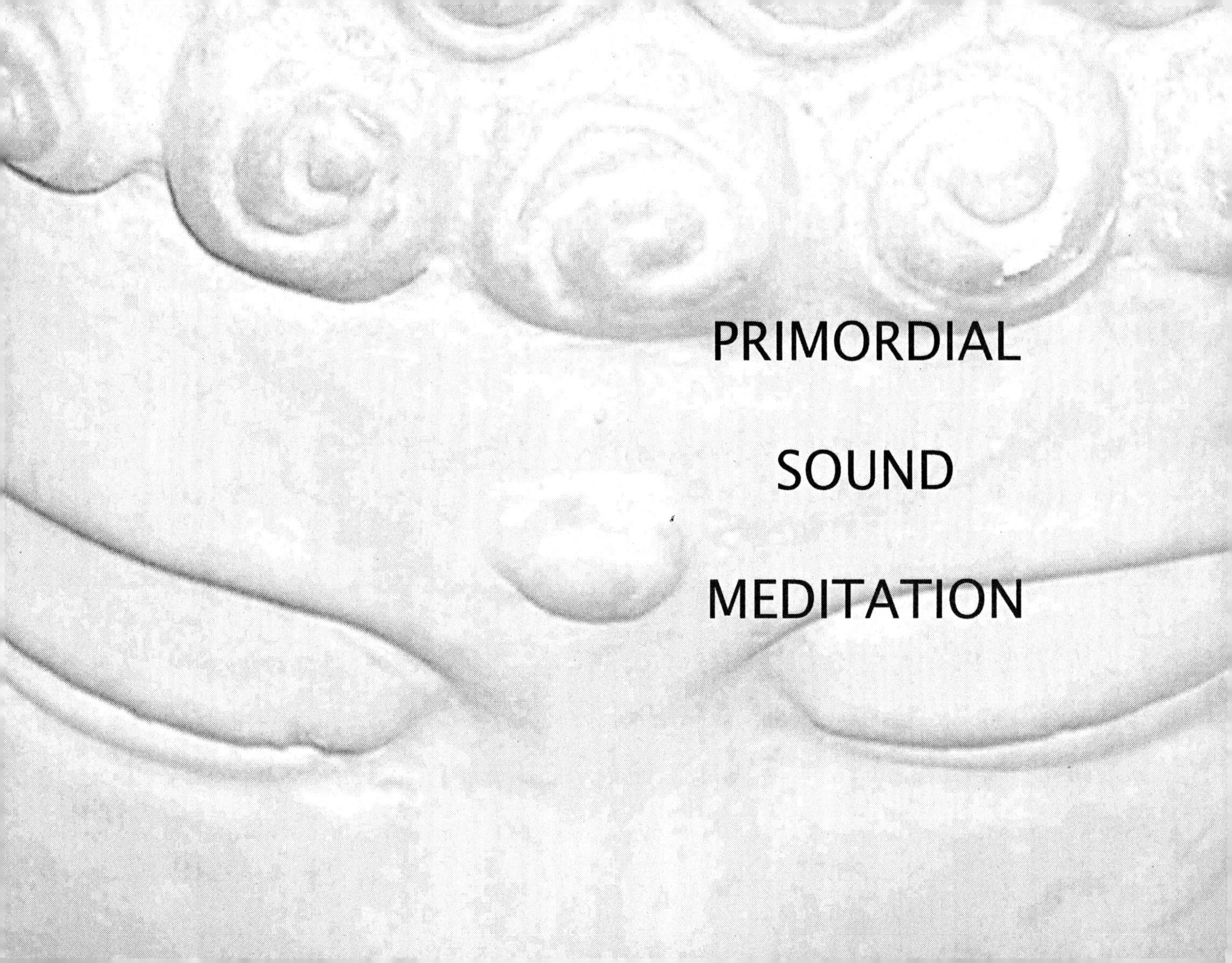
PRIMORDIAL
SOUND
MEDITATION

*Learning to meditate was and is the single most important choice I have ever made. There was a time when my life was dominated by the noise and nonsense of my circumstances. In all its varied forms my identification with and deferral to this noise and nonsense simply reflected the level and extent to which I had lost myself to those circumstances. Meditation allowed me to begin to re-identify with not only the purity of silence but also the real 'me' that was the silence. This state of Self-referral continues to transform all levels of my being. It has become the source my inner healing and the inspiration that helps me navigate through my life.*

*While the other spiritual practices I also use contribute deeply to my overall well being, meditation has been the one constant over the past eighteen years. My life was in crisis when I made the decision to learn to meditate. I had been depressed on and off for most of my childhood and early adulthood. The inner turmoil of these emotional periods peaked in the late eighties with the experience of unrequited love and the loss of my mother to cancer. Twenty-seven years of life had pushed me over the edge and it was the cushioned silence of meditation that caught me, forever changing me in benign ways I will never fully comprehend. Still, I feel compelled to share what I have learned from this profound practice as best I can.*

*I have practiced meditation since the fall of 1989. In 2001, I began a new chapter on my meditative path by first learning and then becoming a Certified Primordial Sound Meditation instructor with Deepak Chopra and the Chopra Centre for Wellbeing.*

*Primordial Sound Meditation is a technique that finds its origions in India. Primordial Sounds – the basic, most essential sounds of nature – are used to disconnect us from the activity of life. These individually selected sounds, known as mantras, are based on the vibration the universe was making at the moment of your birth. Primordial Sound Meditation is easily learned in four short sessions over a period of a few days.*

*There are many scientific and personal documented benefits of the daily practice of meditation. We know that meditators experience increased levels of energy, vitality and renewal. For me it has become a way of navigating the tapestry of my experience. Weaving the thread of silence, I can penetrate the core of my existence.*

*Silence is the playground of our divinity. When the mind is given basic ingredients it will naturally transcend into the silence that is its source. This 'field' of silence cannot be experienced intellectually as, by definition, it is beyond the mind and the cognitive process. But certain meditation techniques allow the mind to settle down enough that we begin to know silence intimately as our own essence and nature.*

*The choice to place our attention on the virtue of silence, which can be found in the gap between our thoughts, allows us to introduce silence not only to our awareness but also into the very activity of our daily lives. The experience of transcendence becomes a practical endeavor. The restoration of stillness ripples through our consciousness, triggering profound effects in all our relationships. Blood pressure is reduced, anxiety is tempered or disappears. Increased brain wave coherence improves our attention span, creativity, memory retrieval and learning abilities. The list becomes a footnote needing no statistical validation for those who engage the silence of meditation on a consistent basis. As our activity becomes saturated with the non-activity of meditation, we begin to access and acquire silent knowledge, a knowledge that lies beyond the rationally thinking, culturally-conditioned hypnosis into which most of us have been indoctrinated.*

*Silence is the source of all inspiration and genius; it is the birthplace of all happiness. Our conscious access to this unbounded domain of awareness provides a resource of unlimited potential, calibrated with accuracy and precision, grounded in the womb of creation itself. Meditation is a vehicle that provides us with a nonverbal, direct experience of truth that lies in the core essence of the worlds' greatest and most sacred teachings. Inherent within this field of silence is the freedom to create any eventuality, a freedom that comes to us as we embody a level of pure awareness that gradually neutralizes the bondage of self imposed, self limiting illusions that lie within the mask of our mortality and material existence.*

*For me the practice of meditation gives life and colour to the heart of my Spirituality. The virtue of silence is the vehicle of inner and outer transformation, an accessible doorway to the mysteries at the heart of creation. When we assess the history of our own and collective stories, it has always been a single attitude, a single idea, a single choice, a single human being that changed the course of destiny. Learning to meditate can be a gift not only for your personal transformation, but also your personal opportunity to influence in the most subtle but powerful way, the course of humanity and the collective consciousness - and that's when the magic really begins.*

*For a more detailed exploration and integration of effortless change in your life,*

*I encourage you to:*

*Learn how to meditate and then practice it on a daily basis.*

*Continue to actively pursue a Spiritual study and journey that speaks deeply to who you are.*

*For more information on locating an instructor for learning Primordial Sound Meditation and other workshops also offered by the Chopra Centre for Wellbeing, please go to:*

**http://www.chopra.com**

*I also encourage you to surf the Alliance for a New Humanity website, it's an international network of people from all walks of life who want to see positive change in the world:*

**http://www.anhglobal.org**

# PERSONAL INSIGHTS

# INITIATIVES

*The Zero Ceiling Society*

Founded in 1997, Zero Ceiling is an unbiased charitable society that offers innovative snowboarding programs to at-risk youth and street youth from Vancouver and Montreal to the slopes of Whistler BC, the Laurentians and Mont Tremblant Quebec. Through adventure-based learning and personal development, Zero Ceiling is making a difference.

The Zero Ceiling mission is to inspire at-risk and disadvantaged youth to experience a productive, fulfilling life through active living, and self-discovery. Programs offered include a flagship Snowboard Instructor Program (SIP), Winter Day Visits, Summer Day Visits, and Peer Mentorship Program. The Snowboard Instructor Program involves carefully selecting a group of up to six youth with our youth agency partners, to participate in an intensive annual week-long course. The selected youth have shown a proven desire to make a change in life and are able to snowboard. If the youth pass the training week, they have the opportunity to move to the mountain to start work as a snowboard instructor, live in staff housing, continue further training and are introduced to a dedicated support network. The youth also receive Level One certification through the Canadian Association of Snowboard Instructors that allows them to work as an instructor anywhere in Canada.

Zero Ceiling also offers winter Snowboarding Day Visits and summer Activity Day Visits. The winter visits provide at-risk youth with a snowboarding lesson on Whistler-Blackcomb and Mont Tremblant. In Whistler, the snowboard instructors are graduates of our SIP, providing powerful and positive role models for the visiting youth. The Summer Activity Day Visits consist of mountain biking, rock climbing, hiking, rafting, skateboarding, wakeboarding or relaxing at a local lake. Each year, Zero Ceiling hosts over 300 youth for Snowboarding Day Visits and Activity Day Visits.

The Peer Mentorship Program trains the previous seasons' graduates of the SIP and members of the community in mentoring skills. They are then assigned to a new graduate to provide them with peer support during their first season in Whistler. This program is self-supporting and led by the Peer

Mentors on a voluntary basis.

In 2007, Zero Ceiling is ramping up for its tenth winter and has hosted well over a thousand youth, some for the day and some for a lifetime. Zero Ceiling looks forward to another decade of helping youth to choose a healthier lifestyle. For more information on The Zero Ceiling Society, please go to:

http://www.zeroceiling.com

# About the author

M Sean Symonds (michael) is a facilitator and self-published author of *A Path of Relationship*, 1998, and *Zen Shredding*, 2007. Both books are about Personal Growth and Spirituality. His training includes Polarity Therapy/counseling [1989], and Rebirthing [1991]. Most recently [2001], he became a certified Primordial Sound Meditation instructor with Deepak Chopra/Chopra Centre. Maintaining a private practice since 1989, Michael facilitates one-on-one and group explorations in personal growth, healing and consciousness. Michael has studied with renowned teachers Dr. Deepak Chopra of the Chopra Centre for Wellbeing and Leonard Orr, founder of the Rebirthing/Conscious Breathing movement. His present studies continue in the area of creativity and teaching based on the work of Deepak Chopra, Steven Wolinsky and the late sage and seer Nisargadatta Maharaj.

In the fall of 2004, Michael moved from Vancouver to Whistler, B.C. realizing that he had found the perfect environment to deepen his personal meditation practice. He became very clear about his intention to mentor others through his creativity, teaching, speaking and writing and his desire to elevate and ennoble the lives of others by inspiring them to nurture the wisdom of their own Souls. Michael invites us to see beyond the concepts of cultural, religious or moral conditioning, encouraging us to ground ourselves in the nature of our true Spirit and Self, which lies beyond the colour of our skin, gender, sexual preference and body/mind.

Michael also loves the indulgence of one on one conversation over great cups of coffee, creativity and snowboarding!

*For more information on Primordial Sound Meditation and other workshops by Michael please go to:*

**http://www.zenshredding.com**

*or*

**http://www.divinityonline.com**

*or visit my personal blog:*

**http://zenshredding.wordpress.com**

My life flows with rhythm and ease.
My breath, my life, my rhythm.
Every breath, every moment, all rhythm.

I listen to my rhythm,
I feel my rhythm,
I touch my rhythm,
I Am the rhythm.

Listen to your rhythm.
Celebrate your rhythm.
Trust your rhythm.
Experience your rhythm.

The rhythm expands,
the rhythm contracts.
Surrender to the rhythm,
I AM.

ISBN 142515887-0
9 781425 158873